SIGHT WORDS in Sentences

Sight Words in Sentences contains all the sight words from SnapWords® Lists A-E, Numbers & Colors in 200 sentences, color-coded by level. 306 high-frequency words including the Dolch List of words, 100 Fountas & Pinnell words and more.

Use for sight word assessment or fluency practice after student has mastered each list of words using the stylized cards. Also aids in comprehension and correct usage of words in context.

CHILD1ST
PUBLICATIONS, LLC

Sight Words in Sentences
Ages 5 and up.

Printed in the United States of America

ISBN: 978-1-936981-18-2

Design: Sarah K Major

Published by Child1st Publications, LLC
800-881-0912 (phone)
888-886-1636 (fax)
www.child1st.com

Other titles by Sarah Major:
Right-Brained Math Series: *Addition & Subtraction Vol 1 & 2, Time, Money, & Measurement, Multiplication & Division, and Fractions. The Illustrated Book of Sounds & Their Spelling Patterns, Alphabet Tales,* Easy-for-Me™ Reading Program, and the Easy-for-Me™ Children's Readers. Other educational work: Child1st SnapWords®.

TABLE OF CONTENTS

ABOUT THIS BOOK

Content:

Sections are color-coded to match SnapWords® Lists A-E colors and symbols. Each section contains only the sight words listed on each section page, with the addition of some number and color words and the following words:

Level A	Level B	Level C	Level D	Level E
ball	book	kids	bikes	bad
cap/caps	cake	pets	door	cars
cat/cats	house	story	friends	park
dad	pizza		river	trip
dog	toys		street	
home			sun	
Mom				

Suggested uses for *Sight Words in Sentences:*

Independent Practice:	*Assessments:*	*Writing Prompts:*
When a child believes they know a sight word list, let them review the words using this book in a reading center or at home with a parent. Allow them access to the corresponding SnapWords®* so they can look up a word they might not remember.	After a child has used this book to check themselves, have them ask a partner to listen to them read the section (A, B, C, etc.). Once a student listener has been through the sentences with them, the teacher may use this book to do a final listening assessment.	*Sight Words in Sentences* is great for enhancing comprehension, reinforcing correct word usage, and for writing prompts. Many of the sentences allude to a story that will inspire a child to write and then draw. For instance, in the green section, "I see two up the tree" might inspire your student to describe two monkeys and write about what they are doing in the tree.

*SnapWords® stylized sight words are essentials for teaching high-frequency words to right-brained learners. Words are embedded in images, and the child's brain snaps a picture of the word and stores it in memory complete with its context and meaning. Later, the image is the vehicle for recall. The word is used in a sentence on the reverse of each card, which enhances comprehension and usage. The body motion provided is another avenue for learning and recall, valuable to kinesthetic learners. SnapWords® are comprised of the Dolch list, the Fountas & Pinnell 500 most frequently recurring words, and 300 Fry words, and more.

For more information about SnapWords® Cards and to download free trial cards, visit **www.child1st.com.**

Section A

SnapWords® List A:

a
an
and
are
as
at
back
big
but
by
call
can
come
did
do
down
for
get
go
has
have
he
help
here
hi
his
I
if
in
is
it
jump
like
little
look
make
me
my
no
not
now
on
or
out
play
ran
said
see
sit
so
stop
the
this
to
up
want
we
will
you

You and I are at home.

Are you in the big, blue one?

I will go up but will not come down.

Come and sit by me.

I can not call for help now.

Will you do this for me as you go?

Come down here. Do not go up.

The dog and an orange cat ran.

Stop by at three so we can play.

Do not make me look for you!

No, I did not call, but I ran out!

Come, make a yellow one now.

Four or five will get to go.

I have green, but you have red.

He has a yellow one.

I want help on this!

His dad is back here now!

Can it jump like my little dog?

He has a big, red ball.

He said, “Did you do this?”

I see two or three up here.

Four or five will look for me.

Six will want to go.

I have his seven little cats.

Look out! No one ran.

Come on! We can play now!

I will call to see if he can play.

Mom said, “Do you want to stop?”

Can you see this is not so big?

We ran by the little, white cats.

I said, "Hi. Can I sit down here?"

Look! I can jump like you.

Now we can get out and play.

Two caps are gold and gray.

I want a pink or purple cap.

I want to go up.

Go see if it is in here.

Is it on my little dog?

Hi! Here we are!

We will jump back a little.

Section B

SnapWords® List B:

about
all
am
any
ask
ate
away
be
cut
eat
fast
fly
from
funny
gave
good
got
him
into
its
just
last
let
many
may
must
new
of
our
pull
put
read
run
saw
say
she
show
sing
still
take
tell
than
that
them
then
they
too
took
try
us
went
what
when
who
why
with
work
yes
your

Read and then sing all about it.

Run away fast from the black cat!

Why did you ask for any of our work?

I just cut the good cake to eat!

I saw that the last one got into its home.

I just gave him a funny book!

I saw him run to read the new book.

Show me what you put on it.

They took pizza and then ate it all.

Who wants to pull this with us?

I will ask, “What is your work?”

Eight of us went when you called.

He may let many of us fly it, too.

We must put all of our new toys away.

I still say she will show us ten books.

Tell them to take the toys home.

I am still bigger than you are.

He went away; then they took nine toys.

I will say why we got into the brown house!

I got away from the black dog!

We will run fast from the dog!

Try and cut the cake for us to eat!

Yes, I gave him a good pizza!

Let me try to be still just for your last show!

What will you try that is new?

When did you get your new toy?

Who went with them to pull it?

Why did you say yes to them?

I took them home to fly and they will be good here.

Will you be here? I will tell about any funny books I read.

Ask me if you eat that pizza!

You must try the new toy!

My dog will be bigger than my cat.

Many of us may read the new book.

I saw them take its toy.

She can show you that they ate it.

When they went, they took it, too.

I will ask, “May I cut the last good one?

She will sing all about it if I am here.

Dad took them to work with him.

Section C

SnapWords® List C: 

after
again
another
around
before
began
better
bring
came
cold
day
didn't
does
don't
far
find
first
found
give
giving
going
gone
had
hard
her
hold
how
kind
know
live
long
made
man
more
much
never
next
off
oh
old
other
over
own
pick
ride
some
soon
there
these
think
those
told
under
very
walk
was
were
where
which

I will run around again after you do.

Go first before you pick another one.

They came and began to work this day.

It is a cold day so you had better bring a cap.

Didn't he give you a toy he found?

Does she find her dog hard to hold?

First I know I must find my mom.

These kids will bring those toys.

How kind of you to think
about giving!

Let us go around one more house.

I don't live very far away; does he?

Which toys were you going to bring next?

Don't go so far again!

I was going, but he was long gone.

I know how kind the man is!

She made much more than he did!

I will never get her off the next ride!

Oh! Look over there at the other ride!

I had better not bring some old pizza!

I was going to call again soon after she had gone.

We came in; it was cold out there!

Before I began to eat much,
I worked under the house.

Walk under this long one very fast.

He works where the silver ones
are made.

I own some old toys. I want to pick
new ones.

I think these will soon go under.

I told those kids to walk, not ride!

Those kids will walk very fast
over the other one!

Oh! I told you where we were.

Which of you likes what I made?

I think these are all there are now.

Those kids told the man a very long story.

I will give the book I found to him another day.

Oh! Next I will take off my other old cap.

Soon I will own some more pets.

I didn’t know how kind the man was!

I know I will never live here before I go over.

I know you will never live around another dog that is hard to hold.

It is never hard for her to hold it.

I am giving her a better ride soon.

Section D

SnapWords® List D:

across
always
animal
been
best
both
buy
clean
close
could
done
draw
even
every
fall
full
goes
grow
high
hot
hurt
I'm
keep
laugh
leave
left
light
mean
might
most
myself
near
need
once
only
open
pretty
right
round
same
short
should
sleep
small
start
their
today
turn
upon
use
warm
well
while
would
yet

I will go across the full river today.

We have always been best friends.

Both of us could close the door.

Draw every one, and I will even laugh!

It will start small but will grow full and high.

Keep the books when you are done.

I have always been the best at play!

I might get hurt if I fall upon the street when I turn.

Both of them will use their new bikes.

I could have done that well, too!

You should not be mean to your friend.

Start small, then let it grow high up!

I'm hot so I might need to leave.

Most of the light had left the fall day.

I need you to not be mean near me!

It is all right to only open it once.

All six animals are the same: pretty, short, and round.

All ten should start their work the same day.

It is their turn to buy a new, clean ball today.

Six small cats could use all of that.

I am always warm while I work.

I have even done the most work by myself.

Will the short one fall and get hurt while you sleep?

It is pretty, light, and goes left and right well.

I'm warm when I'm upon the house.

It is your turn to use the bike, but don't keep it.

It always goes well while you are around.

Would you want to leave yet?

He asked if I would go across by myself yet.

I should clean up before I sleep!

Should you buy that small, round one?

Once you open it, it will not be the same.

I might draw one for my best friends.

I am too hot to turn every one over.

I will only say this once: close the door!

Are you done with that book yet?

The best animal is clean, pretty, and near me.

He should sleep a short while today.

She always goes across every river.

The full sun is high and hot.

Section E

SnapWords® List E:

accident
basement
because
bicycle
breath
careful
carry
certainly
clapped
company
decide
different
drink
enough
father
flapping
giggle
heard
hitch
hundred
husband
imagine
indeed
instant
it's
mother
passenger
playmate
pleasant
please
pleasure
prize
realized
shall
stove
struggled
stuck
stumbled
thank
thought
through
together
tomorrow
toward
twice
wash
whole
willing
wish
wonderful
write

They had an accident in our basement twice!

I was careful to carry them because they were full.

Mother, he certainly does have bad breath!

Our company clapped when I was on my bicycle.

I can not decide what is different about this drink!

I heard eight kids giggle, and that was enough!

The passenger and I had a pleasant trip together.

Please hitch a hundred cars together tomorrow.

I certainly can not decide which one to drink!

I wish you were willing to wash your whole bicycle!

I imagine it's very pleasant in the basement now!

I realized he was careful to carry them to the stove.

The husband thought he heard the hitch flapping.

I imagine we must have a hundred books now!

The passenger needs a playmate this instant!

It was a pleasure to give the dog its prize.

I realized it was pleasant as I went toward the park.

Father struggled to get the stove in the house. It got stuck.

That company got the prize because it’s wonderful indeed.

She stumbled through the door and got stuck right after.

They struggled to read the whole book together twice.

Tomorrow we can make a different instant drink for Mother.

Her husband imagined he heard a big accident.

He said, “Yes, indeed. There was an accident!”

We all stumbled toward home together.

We thought we would go through the park.

I got stuck twice as I went toward the house.

I shall write to thank my wonderful father and mother.

Tomorrow I shall be willing to write it twice.

I wish you were willing to wash the whole stove.

Mother and Father think I'm wonderful, thank you!

I certainly will keep you company with pleasure.

Please! Eight different dogs is enough!

I shall be with you in an instant!

They start flapping because she giggles.

We thought it through together.

I realized I shall indeed get the prize.

I thought we could go through there.

We will go toward home tomorrow.

I am willing to wash the whole house twice.

RELATED PRODUCT

306 SnapWords® Kit

SnapWords® picture sight words are essentials in helping visual learners and young children learn to read more easily.

Do you know a struggling reader? Is your child learning to read? Easy to teach and a snap to learn, the SnapWords® in the Essentials Kit are the foundation for frustration-free reading for children.

This Kit contains the most important words students will learn because of how frequently these words appear in books children read.

Two teaching resources are included for free.

COMPANION PRODUCT

SnapWords® 306 Student Kit

The challenge of meeting each of your students where they are and bringing them to their highest potential is a very real one. Hands-on, independent activities that reinforce and practice what you have taught will make this happen.

It isn't practical for students to use your teaching materials, so the SnapWords® 306 Student Kit supplies heavily laminated, student-sized versions of your teaching cards, leaving your tools available for your own use.

Use this Kit with 306 SnapWords® Teaching Cards or the SnapWords® Classroom Kit.

Find the SnapWords 306 Student Kit at child1st.com.

ABOUT CHILD1ST PUBLICATIONS

Core Beliefs:

We believe every child can learn, that many learning failures are avoidable, and that a label assigned doesn't have to be a life sentence. We believe brains are made to learn, they love to learn, and in most cases they will learn when conditions are right. We also believe that once the gaps in their understanding are bridged, children will progress rapidly.

Product designers at Child1st look at children first to discover how they learn most naturally. We integrate explicit phonics instruction with specific strategies (visuals, movement, storytelling, humor, rhyme, and patterns) to engage children with an array of learning strengths. Teach smarter, more efficiently, and with confidence.

Background:

After many years teaching everything from preschool to college and developing products along the way to meet observed needs, Sarah Major resigned from fulltime teaching in 2006 in order to devote herself to Child1st. What began as a small business in her Florida home quickly grew, gaining friends and customers all over the world.

Contact Us:

Web: www.child1st.com
Phone: 800-881-0912
Email: info@child1st.com